MONSTER SCHOOL

Garry Kilworth

Illustrated by Scoular Anderson

A & C Black • London

The comix series ...

Aargh, it's an Alien! · Karen Wallace
Agent Spike and the Vegetables of Doom · Mark Burgess
Archie's Amazing Game · Michael Hardcastle
Arf and the Greedy Grabber · Philip Wooderson
Arf and the Metal Detector · Philip Wooderson
Arf and the Three Dogs · Philip Wooderson
Freddy's Fox · Anthony Masters
A Ghost Behind the Stars · Chris Powling
The Goose Who Knew Too Much · Peter Utton
Henry's Magic Powers · Peter Utton
Hot Air · Anthony Masters
Jack's Tree · Georgia Byng
Joker · Anthony Masters
Mr Potts the Potty Teacher · Colin West
Monster School · Garry Kilworth
The Planet Machine · Steve Bowkett
Please Don't Eat my Sister! · Caroline Pitcher
Sam's Dream · Michael Hardcastle
Uncle Tom's Pterodactyl · Colin West
Yikes, it's a Yeti! · Karen Wallace

First published in paperback 2002. Reprinted 2004
First published in hardback 2002 by A & C Black Publishers Ltd
37 Soho Square, London W1D 3QZ
www.acblack.com

Text copyright © 2002 Garry Kilworth
Illustrations copyright © 2002 Scoular Anderson

The rights of Garry Kilworth and Scoular Anderson to be identified
as author and illustrator of this work have been asserted by them in
accordance with the Copyrights, Designs and Patents Act 1988.

ISBN 0-7136-6098-8

A CIP catalogue for this book is available from the
British Library.

Printed and bound in Spain by G. Z. Printek, Bilbao

CHAPTER ONE

Mrs Knocker was looking through the 'School Year Book' for a suitable boarding school for her son Tommy.

Tommy's dad had gone to work in Canada and his mum was joining him for a while, so Tommy had to stay for one term at a boarding school.

Tommy's mum was a bit short-sighted.

Ah, this is what I'm looking for, 'Kraken High School – the best school in the country.'

Three weeks later Tommy found himself on the train to Hobbly-Under-Tayker.

When the train pulled in, he saw a car waiting for him with an odd-looking driver.

The car was an old black hearse and the man behind the wheel was as thin as a skeleton. He had large bulging eyes and wore a black top hat and overcoat.

My name is Igor.

Igor looked very old and, what was more, Tommy noticed he had a metal claw instead of a right hand.

He began to get nervous.

Tommy shared his seat with a coffin, from which grunting noises came when they went over bumps.

On the way through the wood they met a pedestrian crossing a bridge. The man shouted a warning to Tommy.

Tommy began to wonder what he'd got himself into.

The driver started singing.

I love my school at Hobb-er-ly, where the hangman's rope swings daily...

When they entered the grounds the car backfired, several times, making a noise like gunshots.

As the hearse passed through the gates clouds of disturbed bats swarmed up into the heavens from the turrets.

Not as good as the jungle gym at my last school.

Tommy spotted the school flag flying from the tallest turret showing a severed boar's head stuck on a sharpened post.

CHAPTER TWO

After the hearse had driven away, Tommy was left with his suitcase on the steps to the main entrance. There was a rope for the doorbell, which led to some bells high above.

Tommy pulled the rope.

CLANG! CLANG!

THE BELLS! THE BELLS!

Tommy caught a glimpse of an ugly hunchback.

The huge doors creaked open and a wizened old woman with spiders in her hair stood there. She was rubbing her eyes as if she had just got out of bed.

Yes?

Are you the matron? I'm a new pupil, Tommy Knocker. I'm expected.

Tommy was led through gloomy halls covered with weird wallhangings and ornaments.

The whole place was as silent as the grave. There were no pupils anywhere.

Did you have to arrive in the middle of the day, disturbing everyone's sleep?

Some of the names of the school's Old Head Boys caught Tommy's eye.

KRAKEN
OLD HEAD BOYS

DRACULA
GRENDEL
KRAKEN
OLD NICK
CYCLOPS

He was taken to a waiting room outside the school Head's study and told to wait until he was called.

Tommy waited — and waited — and waited — until it was midnight.

YAWN!

ZZZZZZ

Then the whole school came alive with...

...lots of noise.

SHRIEK!

HOWOOOOL!

He was called into the Head's study. Ghastly instruments of torture hung on the walls.

The Head of the school was just that! A large severed head on a plate. He looked Tommy up and down.

Looking at the walls, dark as sin, Tommy saw things crawling in and out of them. He shuddered.

The Head said that Tommy could stay for the term.

Tommy was then thrust out into the corridor which was full of young monsters: hellhounds, vampires, Frankenstein creations, werewolves, ghouls, zombies. They stared at Tommy and Tommy stared back.

One of the monsters, a teenage vampire, came over to Tommy and smiled.

The vampire offered his hand. He glanced at Tommy's neck.

CHAPTER THREE

For his first lesson, Tommy attended the vampires' class. They were having an anatomy lesson. On the board was a diagram of a human body, showing the main arteries.

They practised their biting technique on blood oranges.

Tommy tried it and left big teeth marks on the orange skin, whereas the other vampires left little pin pricks. He got 2 out of 10 for his efforts.

Extra homework for you, Knocker!

When Tommy tried to rear up with his jacket for a cloak, the other young vampires laughed.

Never mind, they'll find somewhere for you.

Next he was put into a werewolf class. He tried sticking hair on his face to look like the other werewolves, but it didn't quite work out...

Tommy fared better in the ghoul class. This time he put some flour on his face to make himself look bloodless and adopted a shambling gait. But the other ghouls laughed anyway because he was so short.

When morning came they went to the dining room for supper. There were entrails, throbbing hearts and dishes full of eyeballs. The vampires and werewolves all had mugs of hot blood from an urn. The zombies were eating rotten flesh.

What am I going to eat?

Any cornflakes?

Any bacon and eggs?

Toast?

In the end Tommy opted for the yeti special of yak meat rashers fried in goat's butter. It was all extremely chewy.

After supper they sang the school song —

We are the monsters who hide under beds,
We like to scare people out of their heads,
We like to jump out of cupboards at night,
And give little children a terrible fright!
Kraken! Kraken! Kraken!

Sucer took Tommy to his bed in the dorm.

Tommy was getting very tired after being up all night long. He couldn't wait to curl up and sleep.

I bet you'll sleep like the dead tonight.

Tommy's bed was a coffin half-filled with grave earth. There were worms still crawling through it. He lay on the earth but found it very difficult to get to sleep.

I've had enough of this!

Tommy went to see Matron and asked for another dorm, away from the vampires. But...

The werewolves howled and gnashed their teeth in their sleep when they had good dreams.

I could howl too, with tiredness.

The swamp monsters wallowed in mire and slime.

You'll have to go. Come back when you can learn to swallow mud without choking.

Tommy finally found a reasonable day's sleep with the Egyptian mummies. Luckily there was an empty sarcophagus going.

CHAPTER FOUR

As the term went on, Tommy settled very well. The cook ordered in some ordinary food especially for him.

He made his sarcophagus comfortable with some thick blankets and he got used to sleeping in the day, rather than the night.

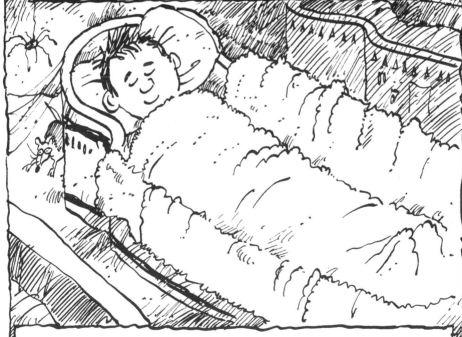

He learned to howl like the werewolves and scream like the banshees, so he joined the school choir.

When he wrote to his parents to tell them he was in the choir they were amazed. He had shown no talent for singing before now.

CHAPTER FIVE

One day the Head received a letter from nearby St Sebastian's School for Boys and Girls.

Kraken School was being challenged to a Sports Day. The Head wondered what to do. None of the monsters had done any sport before. No one in the school really knew what it was all about.

My pupils are good at frightening people to death. We can give people heart attacks, but can we beat them at running I wonder?

What about young Tommy? Surely he knows all about sport – he is a human, after all.

In the school hall, where Tommy was lost amongst the hordes of monsters, he was called forward to meet the Head.

Can you organise a Sports Day for us, Tommy? These people at St Sebastian's think they're the skeleton's knees and keep bragging about how they'll leave us standing.

Of course! Piece of cake!

CHAPTER SIX

Over the next few days Tommy spent a lot of time drawing up lists, organising people (and bodies) and ordering new sports equipment.

Training sessions weren't easy though. The zombies insisted on going into the track races and shambled slowly.

The vampires kept tripping over their cloaks (and the limbs the zombies had dropped on the track).

The ghouls threw their own heads in the shot put instead of the shot itself.

It was chaos.

Tommy gradually began to sort out the mess and some real training started.

Monsters began tapping on Tommy's sarcophagus in the middle of the day to ask him questions, as they began to take the whole thing more seriously.

Can I hop, skip and crunch?

The Head told him, 'We're relying on you.'

CHAPTER SEVEN

Finally the day of the Sports Challenge arrived. Sucer was yawning, showing his fangs. Tommy was nervous.

I don't know how we're going to stay awake all day.

Make sure the others get into their sports gear, you know they hate clothes.

Sucer supervised the warming-up exercises in the gym.

The bus from St Sebastian's arrived.

The faces of the girls and boys in their smart uniforms peered out in horror as they saw Kraken School for the first time.

Look at this lot!

Ghouls and zombies greeted them off the bus and led them to the changing rooms.

The boys and girls were introduced to their opponents for the first time. They were overawed to begin with but the captains soon rallied their forces.

We'll beat this lot. They'll be tripping over their tails and getting their wings caught in their legs! No problem, St Seb's!

The teams paraded out onto the sports field. The monsters looked a bit awkward in their gear, while St Seb's competitors looked the business. There was much flag and banner waving.

ST SEBASTIAN'S

WINNERS
OF
SCHOOL
SPORTS –
1990
1991
1992
1993
1994
1995

The Head was brought out on a silver platter by a floating severed hand and was introduced to the Head of St Sebastian's, a formidable-looking lady in tweeds.

She went to shake hands but then realised Kraken's Head had nothing to shake with.

The severed hand was quick to react.

Can I meet your school coach?

43

The first events of the programme were throwing the discus, throwing the hammer and putting the shot.

Tommy used his best Frankenstein's monster, his fittest mummy and his strongest zombie.

Frankenstein's monster won the discus...

...but the mummy threw the hammer the wrong way as he couldn't see through his swaddling bandages...

...and the zombie once again threw his own bonce in place of the shot.

If only I could keep my head, I think I could be good at this.

Next came the werewolves against boys and girls in the running races and hurdles.

The werewolves insisted on checking the starting pistol.

46

The werewolves won by a good margin, being fast runners and good at leaping over the hurdles.

The St Seb's competitors won the javelin against the yeti and a bogeyman. Everyone had to dodge the flying missiles that filled the air.

The rah-rah boys and girls, cheerleaders from St Seb's, did their yelling.

Kraken's cheerleaders consisted of banshees and bogeymen.

The high jump was won by two young witches assisted by their brooms.

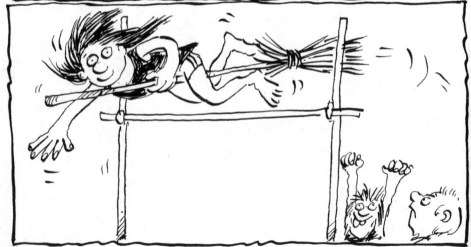

We swept away all opposition.

The steeplechase had several entrants from both schools. From Kraken there were two swamp monsters and Sucer.

The swamp monsters did particularly well because Tommy had made the water jumps very deep. Flesh-eating plants, like venus flytraps, made the monsters feel at home.

To the children from St Seb's, the water jumps looked like black lagoons. How were they going to get across these muddy crocodile-and-piranha-infested waters?

The boys and girls had to swim for their lives, but the swamp monsters got across easily and won. Sucer had been kept at the back by a sneaky St Seb's girl...

The vampires won the pole vault, assisted by their bat-wing cloaks.

St Seb's won the diving competitions in the swimming pool, despite the fact it was filled with swampwater.

GLOOP

SLURP

One of the last events was the swimming race. St Seb's put forward their best swimmer, a tall youth with goggles and a shaven head. No one appeared for Kraken.

A walk-over. Or should it be swim-over?

Mystified, the boy crouched on the diving block and dived in at the sound of the gun...

...only to find he was racing against a young Loch Nessie, already in the water.

It was an exciting race.

The boy was good, but was beaten by a fin.

Finally, it came down to the triple-jump. Several hop-skip-jumpers went from either team, until the score was 40 points each.

The last two to jump were Tommy and a tall boy from St Seb's. It was all up to them!

St Seb's went first.

WHOOSH!

A long triple jump.

But then Tommy flew down the lane — hopped — skipped — jumped...

...and beat his opponent by two centimetres.

There was tea in a tent after the games. Kraken had put on a good feast. There was a buffet for St Seb's with cakes and sandwiches. For the monsters there were plenty of treats.

A cup brought by St Seb's was presented to Tommy on behalf of his teams. Kraken gave the St Seb's coach a gruesome cup made from a skull dripping with slime. Everyone appeared satisfied with the day's events.

The St Seb's bus left as Tommy was being carried on the shoulders of the monsters around the school grounds.

CHAPTER EIGHT

Very soon though, Tommy's last day came. His mum arrived first thing in the morning. Tommy was relieved that his schoolmates would be going to bed when his mum turned up, but he was also sad they wouldn't be seeing him off.

What's that?

Tommy was wearing a bloodsoaked rag pinned to his chest.

School colours. I was the captain of the athletics team and I lead them all to victory over St Sebastian's.

Well, next time you get a nose bleed, dear, use a tissue.

Tommy asked his mother what sport they played in Canada.

Ice hockey, I think dear.

Hmm, I'll have to ask the yetis to get me some tips.

His mother looked at him strangely.

What on earth is he talking about?

Tommy turned to take one last look at Kraken — just in case...